Big Book of BEADED ORNAMENTS

Transform your Christmas tree into a "bead-dazzler" with beautiful beaded ornaments that you make yourself! From fun and funky to elegant and ornate, we have trims to suit everyone's personal style. The 71 designs range in skill level from easy to advanced, so the whole family can join in on the merry-making. Whether you choose old-fashioned favorites — which we've updated with simpler techniques — or something new and unique, our step-by-step instructions, full-color photographs, and easy-to-understand figures will make creating these eye-catching baubles a snap! Detailed supply lists help you craft ornaments exactly like ours, or you can choose freeform designs to assemble with your own bead selections.

Contents

Leisure Arts • Maumelle, Arkansas

Beaded Elegance

If you prefer ornaments with an air of elegance, you'll love these beaded beauties! The regal designs include beaded patterns, collars, and overlays.

Colorful Collar

1. Read **Beading Basics**, pgs. 58-60, and refer to **Beading Diagrams**, pg. 56, to complete each row. Cut a $1^1/_2$ yd length of thread, adding new thread as needed.

2. For Row 1, leaving a 3" tail and locking first bead in place, thread one bicone bead and three seed beads. Repeat pattern eight more times. Thread needle through locking bead twice to secure Row 1; place on ornament.

3. For Row 2, thread eight seed beads, one bicone bead, and eight seed beads. Thread needle through the next bicone bead in Row 1 to complete scallop. Repeat pattern eight more times. Thread needle through eight seed beads and one bicone bead in Row 2.

4. For Row 3, thread five bicone beads. Thread needle through next bicone bead in Row 2 to complete scallop. Repeat pattern eight more times. Thread needle through three bicone beads in Row 3.

5. For Row 4, thread five bicone beads. Skip five bicone beads in Row 3 and thread needle through next bicone bead to complete scallop. Repeat pattern eight more times. Thread needle through three bicone beads in Row 4.

6. For Row 5, thread 10 seed beads, one bicone bead, and 10 seed beads. Skip five bicone beads in Row 4 and thread needle through next bicone bead to complete scallop. Repeat pattern eight more times. Thread needle through 10 seed beads and one bicone bead in Row 5.

7. For Row 6, thread seven bicone beads. Thread needle through next bicone bead in Row 5 to complete scallop. Repeat pattern eight more times. Thread needle through four bicone beads in Row 6.

8. For Row 7, thread seven bicone beads. Skip seven bicone beads in Row 6 and thread needle through next bicone bead to complete scallop. Repeat pattern eight more times.

9. For long dangle, refer to **Beading Diagrams**, pg. 57, to thread seed beads and bicone beads, then to double back through dangle and bicone bead in Row 7. Thread needle through four bicone beads in Row 7.

10. For short dangle, thread one seed bead, one bicone bead, and one teardrop bead. Double back through dangle and bicone bead in Row 7. Thread needle through four bicone beads in Row 7.

11. Repeat Steps 9 and 10 eight more times. Thread needle through last bicone bead twice to lock in place. Secure thread ends to complete collar.

Materials

- ❖ $3^1/_4$" dia. matte green glass ball ornament
- ❖ light green seed beads (522)
- ❖ 4mm multicolored transparent bicone beads (297)
- ❖ 13.5 x 6.5mm crystal AB teardrop beads (9)
- ❖ beading needle
- ❖ beading thread
- ❖ liquid fray preventative

Note: We used Blue Moon light green luster seed beads and fine ash thread.

Gold Collar

1. Read **Beading Basics**, pgs. 58-60, and refer to **Beading Diagrams**, pg. 54, to complete each row. Cut a $1^1/_2$ yd length of thread, adding new thread as needed.

2. For Row 1, leaving a 3" tail and locking first bead in place, thread one 3mm bead and one bugle bead. Repeat pattern nine more times. Thread needle through locking bead twice to secure Row 1; place on ornament.

3. For Row 2, thread eight 3mm beads, one 4mm bead, and eight 3mm beads. Skip one 3mm bead in Row 1 and thread needle through the next to complete scallop. Repeat pattern four more times. Pass needle around locking bead in Row 1; double back through last four 3mm beads in Row 2.

4. For first half scallop in Row 3, thread one 3mm bead, one bugle bead, one 3mm bead, one bugle bead, and one 3mm bead.

5. For dangle, thread three 3mm beads, two 4mm beads, one 5mm bead, and one 6mm bead. Thread one 3mm bead; double back through dangle beads.

6. For second half scallop in Row 3, repeat pattern in Step 4. Thread needle through four 3mm beads on next scallop in Row 2, bringing needle out at top of collar. Thread through bugle bead, 3mm bead, and bugle bead in Row 1, then thread through last four 3mm beads in Row 2.

7. Repeat Steps 4-6 four more times. Thread needle through half scallop in Row 3 to dangle.

8. For Row 4, skip dangle, and thread needle through 3mm bead and bugle bead on next half scallop. Thread eight 3mm beads, one 5mm bead, and eight 3mm beads. Thread needle through second bugle bead on half scallop in Row 3, then thread through 3mm bead to dangle. Repeat pattern four more times.

9. Thread needle through top dangle bead twice to lock in place. Secure thread ends to complete collar.

Materials

- $3^1/_4$" dia. red glass ball ornament
- 3mm gold round beads (220)
- 4.5mm gold bugle beads (30)
- 4mm gold round beads (15)
- 5mm gold round beads (10)
- 6mm gold round beads (5)
- beading needle
- beading thread
- liquid fray preventative

Note: We used Blue Moon fine ash thread.

Green And Gold Collar

1. Read **Beading Basics**, pgs. 58-60, and refer to **Beading Diagrams**, pg. 55, to complete each row. Cut a $1^{1}/_{2}$ yd length of thread, adding new thread as needed.

2. For Row 1, leaving a 3" tail and locking first bead in place, thread one flower bead and 15 gold petite beads. Repeat pattern three more times. Thread needle through locking bead twice to secure Row 1; place on ornament.

3. For Row 2, thread one light green bead, one dark green bead, one light green bead, one gold petite bead, one light green bead, and one gold petite bead. Repeat pattern four more times. Thread one light green bead, one dark green bead, and one light green bead. Thread needle through the next flower bead in Row 1 to complete scallop. Repeat entire pattern three more times.

4. For Row 3, thread 24 gold petite beads, one leaf bead, and one dark green bead. Double back through leaf bead. Thread 24 gold petite beads. Thread needle through the next flower bead in Row 1 to complete scallop. Repeat entire pattern three more times. Thread needle through 24 gold petite beads, one leaf bead, and one dark green bead in Row 3. Double back through leaf bead.

5. For Row 4, thread eight gold petite beads, one light green bead, one dark green bead, one light green bead, and eight gold petite beads for first segment. Thread one light green bead, one 4mm gold bead, and one light green bead for center segment. Repeat first segment. Thread needle through the next leaf bead and dark green bead. Double back through leaf bead. Repeat entire pattern three more times.

6. For Row 5, thread beads using pattern from Step 3, completing first segment by threading needle through next 4mm gold bead from Row 4. Continue pattern, completing next segment by threading needle through the next leaf bead and dark green bead. Double back through leaf bead. Repeat entire pattern three more times.

7. Thread needle through first light green bead in Row 5 twice to lock in place. Secure thread ends to complete collar.

Materials

- ❖ $3^{1}/_{4}$" dia. matte gold glass ball ornament
- ❖ gold petite glass beads (500)
- ❖ green flower and leaf beads from bead mixture (4 each)
- ❖ light green frosted glass beads (228)
- ❖ dark green petite glass beads (84)
- ❖ 4mm gold round beads (4)
- ❖ beading needle
- ❖ beading thread
- ❖ liquid fray preventative

Note: We used Blue Moon dark green bead mix and fine ash thread.

Spotted And Striped Ball

Press tape around center of ball; remove paper backing. Follow manufacturer's instructions to press Glue Dots randomly around ball. Place marbles on paper plate. Roll ball in marbles until tape and dots are covered; press marbles firmly to ball.

Materials

- ❖ 2¹/₄" dia. matte green glass ball ornament
- ❖ tiny glass marbles
- ❖ ¹/₄"w PEELnSTICK™ double-sided adhesive tape
- ❖ ¹/₄" dia. Glue Dots™
- ❖ paper plate

Note: We used very tiny gold metallic marbles.

Materials

- ❖ 2¹/₄" dia. matte white glass ball ornament
- ❖ tiny glass marbles
- ❖ ¹/₄"w PEELnSTICK™ double-sided adhesive tape
- ❖ pencil
- ❖ measuring tape
- ❖ paper plate

Note: We used very tiny kelly green and gold metallic marbles and very tiny red and crystal transparent marbles.

Striped Ball

Measure around center of ball and lightly mark eight equal sections. Press tape over each pencil line; remove paper backing. Place gold marbles on paper plate. Roll ball in marbles until tape is covered; press marbles firmly to ball. Cut strips of tape to fit inside four alternate sections, trimming each end to a point; press in place and remove paper backing. Roll ball in crystal marbles until tape is covered; press marbles firmly to ball. Apply kelly green, then red marbles to remaining alternate sections.

Spotted Ball

Following manufacturer's instructions, press Glue Dots randomly around ball. Place tiny glass marbles on paper plate. Roll ball in marbles until dots are covered; press marbles firmly to ball. Tie ribbon in a bow around hanger.

Materials

- ❖ 3¹/₄" dia. matte red glass ball ornament
- ❖ tiny glass marbles
- ❖ ⁵/₈ yds of 1"w wire-edged ribbon
- ❖ ¹/₂" dia. Glue Dots™
- ❖ paper plate

Note: We used very tiny gold metallic marbles.

Decoupage Balls

Tear napkins or tissue paper into small pieces. Use paintbrush to apply glue to small section of ball. Lay pieces of paper over the glue; use paintbrush to smooth paper out. Apply more glue to prevent edges from coming up. Repeat until ball is covered; hang to dry. Apply another thick layer of glue to ball, covering a small section at a time. Place desired size marbles on paper plate. Roll ball in marbles until section is covered; press marbles firmly to ball.

Materials

- ❖ $2^1/_4$" and $3^1/_4$" dia. glass ball ornaments
- ❖ transparent tiny glass marbles
- ❖ paper napkins or tissue paper
- ❖ decoupage glue
- ❖ old paintbrush
- ❖ paper plate

Note: We used large, tiny, and very tiny crystal marbles.

Trimmed Balls

Mark fringe placement on each ball $2^1/_4$" from top of hanger. Allowing space for fringe and working on one half of ball, freehand snowflakes, swirls, stars, or dots with craft glue. While still tacky, hold ornament over a paper plate and pour marbles over glued areas until completely covered; press marbles firmly to ball. Place ball in paper cup to dry. Repeat for other half of ball. When completely dry, press adhesive tape on pencil line and peel off paper backing. Press desired fringe onto tape; trim excess. Glue trim above edge of fringe if desired. Dot raw ends of fringe or trim with glue to prevent fraying.

Materials

- ❖ $3^1/_4$" dia. white, cream, and light green glass ball ornaments
- ❖ tiny glass marbles
- ❖ 12" lengths of purchased beaded fringe (3)
- ❖ 12" length of purchased trim (optional)
- ❖ $^1/_4$"w PEELnSTICK™ double-sided adhesive tape
- ❖ craft glue
- ❖ pencil
- ❖ measuring tape
- ❖ paper plate and cup

Note: We used very tiny gold metallic marbles.

Fun & Funky

The whole family will have fun decorating the tree with these Noel novelties! From angels and icicles to tassels and light-cover ornaments, there's something for everyone!

Lime Angel

1. Read **Beading Basics**, pgs. 58-60.

2. For body, slip seven eye pins onto split ring. On each eye pin, thread one lime bead, one dark red bead, and seven lime beads. Wrap end of each eye pin to secure beads.

3. For backbone, cut a 6" length of wire and wrap one end to secure beads. Thread seven lime beads, one medium light green bead, one lime bead, and one large light green bead for head onto wire. Kink wire above head to secure beads; do not trim excess.

4. For arms, cut a 5" length of wire and wrap one end to secure beads. Thread two lime beads, one dark red bead, and seven lime beads to complete one arm; wrap once around split ring. Placing backbone in center of split ring, wrap arm wire around backbone between large light green bead and lime bead. Wrap wire around opposite side of split ring, leaving four of the eye pins to the front of arm wire. Thread remaining arm beads in reverse of first arm. Wrap wire end to secure beads; trim excess.

5. For each wing, cut a 5" length of wire; wrap one end around top of eye pin just behind arm. Thread three lime beads, bending wire to keep beads in center. Wrap wire end around same eye pin.

6. For skirt, cut a 7" length of wire and wrap one end to secure beads. Thread two lime beads, one bow-shaped bead from light green bead mix, and two lime beads. Thread wire through the bottom loop of eye pin at back of angel. Continue pattern around circle. Wrap wire end around beginning loop to secure; trim excess.

7. For each leg, thread one leaf-shaped bead from light green bead mix, two lime beads, two dark red beads, and 10 lime beads onto head pin. Wrap end through loop at base of backbone to secure.

8. For halo, wrap a 10" length of wire into a cone-shaped coil and thread onto backbone wire above head. Bend a hook on end of backbone wire for hanger.

Materials

- lime and dark red transparent seed beads
- light green bead mix
- 2" eye pins (7)
- 16mm gold split ring
- 20 gauge jewelry wire
- 3" head pins (2)
- tapered paintbrush
- wire cutters
- needle nose pliers

Note: We used Blue Moon light green bead mix.

Single And Triple Snowflakes

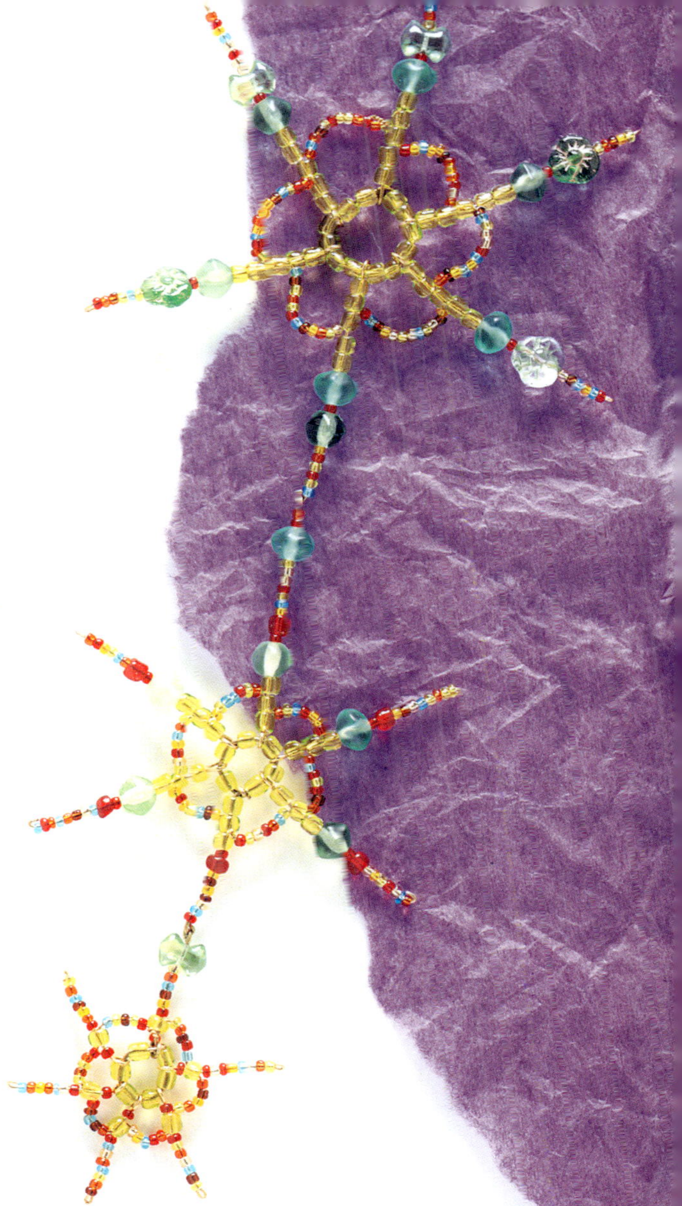

1. Read **Beading Basics**, pgs. 58-60.

2. For single snowflake or top of triple snowflake, cut a 5" length of wire and wrap one end to secure beads. Thread two lime beads and one 2" eye pin on wire; repeat five more times. Wrap wire end around beginning loop to secure; trim excess.

3. For each spoke, thread five lime beads, one large light green bead, one red multi bead, one large light green bead, and five to eight multi beads on eye pin. Wrap end of eye pin to secure beads.

4. For scallops, thread an 8" length of wire through third lime bead from center on one spoke; wrap end to secure. Thread 12 multi beads on wire and thread wire through third lime bead on next spoke; repeat around circle. Wrap wire end around beginning lime bead to secure; trim excess.

5. For hanger, loop a 10" length of monofilament through eye pin at top of snowflake; knot ends.

6. For center of triple snowflake, cut five 2" eye pins to 1½". Cut a 5" length of wire and wrap one end to secure beads. Thread one lime bead and one eye pin on wire. Repeat four more times. Thread one lime bead and 2" eye pin on wire. Wrap wire end around beginning loop to secure; trim excess.

7. For spokes, thread three lime beads, one light green bead, one red multi bead, one dark red bead, and six to eight multi beads on 1½" eye pins. Wrap ends of eye pins to secure beads. On 2" eye pin, thread same beads plus one large light green bead and two multi beads. Wrap end of 2" eye pin around loop of bottom spoke of top snowflake.

8. For scallops, thread a 6" length of wire through second lime bead from center on top spoke; wrap end to secure. Thread six multi beads on wire and thread wire through second lime bead on next spoke; repeat around circle. Wrap wire end around beginning lime bead to secure; trim excess.

9. For bottom of triple snowflake, cut a 4" length of wire and wrap one end to secure beads. Thread one lime bead and one 1" eye pin on wire. Repeat five more times. Wrap wire end around beginning loop to secure; trim excess.

10. For spokes, thread one red multi bead, one lime bead, and six to eight multi beads on five eye pins. Wrap ends of eye pins to secure beads. On sixth eye pin, thread same beads plus one large light green bead. Wrap end of sixth eye pin around loop of bottom spoke of center snowflake.

11. For scallops, thread a 4" length of wire through lime bead on top spoke; wrap end to secure. String five multi beads on wire and thread wire through lime bead on next spoke; repeat around circle. Wrap wire end around beginning lime bead to secure; trim excess.

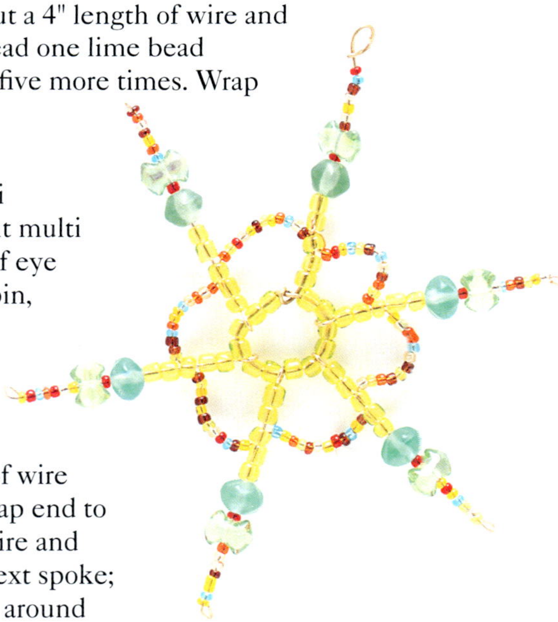

Materials

- ❖ lime transparent seed beads
- ❖ dark red transparent seed beads (Triple Snowflake only)
- ❖ light green bead mix
- ❖ multicolored "multi" transparent silver-lined seed beads
- ❖ 1" eye pins (Triple Snowflake only)
- ❖ 2" eye pins
- ❖ 20 gauge jewelry wire
- ❖ monofilament
- ❖ wire cutters
- ❖ needle nose pliers

Note: We used Blue Moon light green bead mix.

Small Purse

1. Read **Beading Basics**, pgs. 58-60. Apply fray preventative to all knots and trimmed threads.

2. For purse flap, refer to **Beading Diagrams**, pg. 57, and fold one raw edge of ribbon along wrong side of ribbon. Fold ribbon again; glue ends in place.

3. For purse, press remaining raw edge of ribbon 1/4" to wrong side; glue in place. Fold 2" to wrong side again. Overhand stitch sides of purse together, catching one seed bead after each stitch. Knot and trim thread ends.

4. For bottom dangles, cut a 1 yd length of thread. Thread needle; knot ends. Bring needle from inside purse out at bottom left corner.
Dangle 1 – Thread three seed beads; double back through top two beads into purse.
Note: After completing each dangle and threading needle into bottom of purse, bring needle out 1/8" to right of previous bead to begin next dangle.
Dangle 2 – Thread four seed beads; double back through next to last bead. Thread two seed beads, then into purse.
Dangle 3 – Thread five seed beads, one glass bead, and one seed bead; double back through glass and seed beads into purse.
Dangle 4 – Thread nine seed beads, one glass bead, and one seed bead; double back through glass and seed beads into purse.
Dangle 5 – Thread 15 seed beads, one glass bead, and one seed bead; double back through glass and seed beads into purse.
Repeat Dangles 4 through 1. Take needle to inside of bottom right corner of purse; knot and trim thread ends.

5. For purse flap embellishment, fold flap to front of purse. Cut a 1 yd length of thread. Thread needle; knot ends. Bring needle from inside flap out at bottom right corner. Backstitch to point of flap, catching a seed bead with each stitch. Take a small stitch at point to anchor thread. For dangle, thread three seed beads, one glass bead, and one seed bead. Double back through glass bead. Thread three seed beads. Take a small stitch at point and continue adding beaded backstitch to edge of flap. Knot and trim thread ends.

6. For handle, cut a 1 yd length of thread. Thread needle; knot ends. Bring needle from inside purse out at top right corner. Thread seed beads and glass beads to complete one 3 1/2" strand. Take a small stitch at top left corner of purse to anchor thread. Thread seed beads to complete second 3 1/2" strand, running needle through some glass beads on first strand. Knot thread inside top right corner of purse and trim ends.

Materials

- gold transparent rainbow seed beads
- assorted glass beads
- beading needle
- 7" length of 1 1/2"w wire-edged ribbon
- multicolored metallic thread
- liquid fray preventative
- fabric glue

Large Purse

1. Read **Beading Basics**, pgs. 58-60. Apply fray preventative to all knots and trimmed threads.

2. For purse flap, follow Step 2 from **Small Purse**, pg. 18.

3. For purse, press remaining raw edge of ribbon 1/4" to wrong side; glue in place. Fold 3 1/2" to wrong side again. Overhand stitch sides of purse together. Knot and trim thread ends.

4. For bottom dangles, cut a 1 1/2 yd length of thread. Thread needle; knot ends. Bring needle from inside purse out at bottom left corner.
Dangle 1 – Thread nine seed beads, one small pearl, and one seed bead; double back through pearl and five seed beads. Thread four seed beads; stitch to bottom of purse and double back through last bead.
Dangle 2 – Thread 10 seed beads, one small pearl, and one seed bead; double back through pearl and seven seed beads. Thread four seed beads; stitch to bottom of purse and double back through last bead.
Dangle 3 – Thread 13 seed beads, one large pearl, and one seed bead; double back through large pearl and 10 seed beads. Thread four seed beads; stitch to bottom of purse and double back through last bead.
Dangle 4 – Thread 10 seed beads, one glass bead, five seed beads, one large pearl, and one seed bead; double back through large pearl, seed beads, and glass bead. Thread 11 seed beads, then take needle inside bottom of purse approximately 5/8" to right of previous stitch.
Inner Dangle – Bring needle out at previous stitch, threading through first four beads of Dangle 4. Thread four seed beads; stitch to bottom of purse between Dangle 4 stitches and double back through last bead. Thread three seed beads. Thread needle through last four beads of Dangle 4; stitch to bottom of purse and double back through last bead.
Dangles 5 and 6 – Repeat Dangles 3 and 2.
Dangle 7 – Thread eight seed beads, one small pearl, and one seed bead; double back through pearl and five seed beads. Thread four seed beads. Take needle to inside of bottom right corner of purse; knot and trim thread ends.

5. For purse flap embellishment, fold flap to front of purse. Cut a 1 yd length of thread. Thread needle; knot ends. Bring needle from inside flap out at bottom right corner. Thread three seed beads; overhand stitch through flap. Repeat pattern to point of flap. Thread one seed bead, one glass bead, one seed bead, one small pearl, and one seed bead. Double back through small pearl and remaining beads to point. Overhand stitch at point and continue seed bead pattern along edge of flap. Knot and trim thread ends.

6. For handle, cut a 1 1/4 yd length of thread. Thread needle; knot ends. Bring needle from inside purse out at top right corner. Thread seed beads, pearls, and glass beads to complete one 5" strand. Take a small stitch at top left corner to anchor thread. Thread seed beads and small pearl to complete second 5" strand, running needle through some pearls, seed beads, and glass beads on first strand. Knot thread inside top right corner of purse and trim ends.

Materials

- gold transparent rainbow seed beads
- assorted pearl round beads
- assorted glass beads
- beading needle
- 10" length of 2 5/8"w wire-edged ribbon
- multicolored metallic thread
- liquid fray preventative
- fabric glue

Funky Green Ornaments

1. Read **Beading Basics**, pgs. 58-60.

2. For Jellyfish arms, thread beads onto seven head pins. For Hydra and Flying Saucer arms, cut five 7" lengths of 20 gauge wire. Beginning 1" from end of wire, coil or crimp arms. Thread beads onto arms; coil wire to secure beads.

3. For body, cut one 15" length of 20 gauge wire. Beginning 3" from end of wire, crimp or form cone-shaped coils. Thread beads and any wooden items onto wire, kinking wire as needed to hold beads in place. For hanger, bend top of wire; trim excess.

4. To assemble Jellyfish, thread arms through pony bead on body, thread seed bead on end of each arm below pony bead, and wrap wire ends to secure. To assemble Hydra and Flying Saucer, insert arms in large bead on body and hot glue in place. Bend arms to desired shape.

5. To add a bead dangle at bottom of Jellyfish or Flying Saucer body, cut a 2" length of 20 gauge wire. Wrap wire end to secure bead. Thread bead on wire; wrap wire end around bottom of body to secure.

6. To add a beaded collar, thread enough seed beads on 30 gauge wire to wrap around wooden item. Twist wire ends together; trim excess.

Materials

- red and green bead mixes
- 20 gauge gold jewelry wire
- wire cutters
- needle nose pliers
- hot glue gun

Additional Materials

For Hydra (left):

- lime transparent seed beads
- 10mm wooden green bead
- 30 gauge bead wire
- 1" wooden candle cup painted red
- crimper for metal and wire

For Jellyfish (center):

- lime and red transparent seed beads
- 8mm pony bead
- large red glass heart bead
- 3" head pins (7)
- paintbrush with tapered handle

For Flying Saucer (right):

- red transparent seed beads
- 8mm wooden half-ball bead painted light green
- 20mm wooden disc painted dark green
- 30 gauge bead wire
- nail or skewer
- paintbrush with tapered handle

Bead Tassel

1. Read **Beading Basics**, pgs. 58-60. Apply fray preventative to all knots and trimmed threads.

2. For beaded disc, cover wooden disc with tape. Roll disc in seed beads until tape is covered; press beads firmly to disc.

3. For tassel, cut seven 12" lengths of thread. Thread a 2 1/4" to 4 1/2" length of beads on one thread, locking first bead in place. Thread beaded length through disc. Repeat with remaining threads. Knot thread tails together, pulling knot as close to disc as possible.

4. For hanger, trim all but two threads at disc. Run threads through needle and thread three beads above disc. Separate the strands and thread a 1 3/4" length of seed beads onto each strand. Tie strands together to form a loop. Secure thread ends.

Materials

- 30mm wooden disc bead
- bronze seed beads
- glass bead mix
- beading needle
- beading thread
- liquid fray preventative
- 1/4"w PEELnSTICK™ double-sided adhesive tape

Note: We used Blue Moon winter dream transparent bead mix and fine ash thread.

Space-Age Angel

1. Read **Beading Basics**, pgs. 58-60. Allow paints and glue to dry after each application.

2. For wings, drill hole in center top of heart. Apply glue to end of dowel; insert dowel into hole. Paint heart and dowel metallic gold.

3. For head, paint wooden ball flesh. With hole at top and bottom of head, adhere marbles to head using glue thinned with water; press firmly. Glue beads to face for eyes and mouth. Apply glue to remaining end of dowel; insert into bottom of head.

4. For hair, cut two 18" lengths of wire. Thread both wires through clear round bead; fold wires in half with bead at center. Thread assorted beads on each wire end, adding sequins and bending or coiling wire as desired. Wrap wire ends to secure beads; trim excess.

5. For halo, cut an 18" length of wire. Thread one end of wire through clear bead at base of hair; wrap wire end to secure. Bend, then curl wire into a halo. Glue clear bead at base of hair to hole in top of head.

6. For hanger, loop a 10" length of monofilament around hair wire; knot ends.

Materials

- 3 1/2" x 4" wooden heart
- 1" length of 5/16" dia. dowel rod
- 8mm clear round bead
- assorted beads
- 1 1/2" dia. wooden round ball with 5/16" hole
- multicolored tiny glass marbles
- 26 gauge copper wire
- monofilament
- silver round sequins
- metallic gold and flesh acrylic paint
- paintbrush
- craft glue
- nail or skewer
- wire cutters
- needle nose pliers
- drill with 5/16" bit

Colorful Icicles

1. Read **Beading Basics**, pgs. 58-60. Cut a 20" length of desired wire for each icicle.

2. For each icicle, curl or coil end of wire. Thread beads on wire, using larger beads at top and alternating with smaller beads or sequins. Coiling wire as desired, continue adding beads.

3. To finish, coil or wrap wire end to secure beads; trim excess. If desired, loosely coil completed icicle around pencil.

Materials

- assorted beads
- 20-24 gauge metallic wire
- assorted sequins
- nail or skewer
- wire cutters
- needle nose pliers
- pencil (optional)

Light-Cover Ornaments

1. Read **Beading Basics**, pgs. 58-60. Remove top and hanger from each ornament.

2. For each light cover, wrap one end of 18 gauge wire around top of ornament; hot glue in place. Continue wrapping wire, leaving a 2" tail.

3. Beginning 3" from end of 24 gauge wire, coil wire around T-pin three times. Thread bead onto wire, then coil wire around T-pin three more times. Leave $1^1/_2$" of wire straight. Repeat pattern, stopping 3" from end of wire.

4. Hot glue one end of beaded wire to base of ornament top. Wrap wire around ornament randomly; hot glue remaining end to base of ornament top.

5. Slip light cover over one miniature light. Wrap tail of 18 gauge wire around light string to secure.

Materials

- $2^1/_4$" dia. iridescent glass ball ornaments
- string of clear miniature lights
- assorted glass beads
- 18 gauge copper bead wire (11" length per ornament)
- assorted colors of 24 gauge bead wire (9' length per ornament)
- T-pin
- wire cutters
- needle nose pliers
- hot glue gun

Snow And Ice

Refresh your ornament collection with our crystal keepsakes! The frosty trims will add an iridescent sparkle to your Yuletide décor.

Small Sunburst Ball

1. Read **Beading Basics**, pgs. 58-60. Spray paint ball and allow to dry.

2. Load 20 nickel head pins with one silver bead, one rondelle bead, one faceted bead, one silver bead, and one sunburst bead. Push pins into ball, spacing evenly.

3. Load 20 straight pins with one silver bead, one rondelle bead, and one faceted bead. Push pins into ball, spacing evenly.

4. Fill in gaps with straight pins, each loaded with one silver bead and one sunburst bead.

5. Adjust pins as desired and secure. For hanger, fold a 10" length of monofilament into a loop; tie to straight pin. Secure pin in ball.

Materials

- 2" dia. Styrofoam™ ball
- 3mm silver round beads
- 6mm white rondelle beads
- 6mm crystal faceted beads
- 10mm white sunburst beads
- monofilament
- 2" nickel head pins
- straight pins
- Design Master® silver spray paint
- craft glue

Materials

- 1 1/4" dia. Styrofoam™ ball
- 3mm silver round beads
- 6mm white rondelle beads
- 6mm crystal faceted beads
- 10mm white sunburst beads
- monofilament
- 2" nickel head pins
- straight pins
- Design Master® silver spray paint
- craft glue

Mini Sunburst Ball

1. Read **Beading Basics**, pgs. 58-60. Spray paint ball and allow to dry.

2. Load seven nickel head pins with one silver bead, one rondelle bead, one faceted bead, one silver bead, and one sunburst bead. Load seven straight pins with one silver bead, one rondelle bead, and one faceted bead.

3. Push loaded pins around center of ball, alternating pin sizes.

4. Adjust pins as desired and secure. For hanger, fold a 10" length of monofilament into a loop; tie to straight pin. Secure pin in ball.

Sunburst Ball

1. Read **Beading Basics**, pgs. 58-60.

2. Load 20 corsage pins with one 4mm bead, one bugle bead, one 4mm bead, and one sunburst bead. Push pins into ball, spacing evenly.

3. Load 50 corsage pins with one bugle bead and one sequin. Push pins into ball, spacing evenly.

4. Fill in gaps with straight pins, each loaded with one sequin.

5. Adjust pins as desired and secure. For hanger, fold a 10" length of monofilament into a loop; tie to straight pin. Secure pin in ball.

Materials

- 3" dia. Styrofoam™ ball
- 4mm white round beads
- 9mm clear silver-lined bugle beads
- 25mm white sunburst beads
- monofilament
- corsage pins
- white round-headed straight pins
- 8mm white opalescent round sequins
- craft glue

Materials

- crystal twisted bugle beads (42)
- 5mm transparent bicone beads (54)
- 6 x 19mm AB spaghetti pearl beads (6)
- 32 gauge bead wire
- wire cutters
- needle nose pliers

Beaded Snowflake A

1. Read **Beading Basics**, pgs. 58-60.

2. For center circle, work counterclockwise. Leave a 3" tail and thread one bugle bead on a $1^1/_2$ yd length of wire. Thread one bicone bead. Repeat pattern five more times. Twist tail around wire, close to last bead; trim tail.

3. For small points, thread one bugle, one bicone, and one bugle bead. Thread wire through next bicone bead on center circle. Repeat pattern five more times. Thread wire through bugle and bicone beads on first small point.

4. For medium points, thread two bugle, one bicone, and two bugle beads. Thread wire through bicone bead on next small point. Repeat pattern five more times.

5. For large points, thread one spaghetti bead and three bicone beads. Thread wire through bicone bead on next medium point. Thread three bicone beads and one spaghetti bead. Thread wire through bicone bead on next small point. Double back through spaghetti bead and continue pattern until snowflake is completed. Thread wire through last bead twice, then through next three beads; trim excess.

6. For hanger, fold a 6" length of wire into a loop; thread one end through bicone bead on one medium point. Twist wire ends; trim excess.

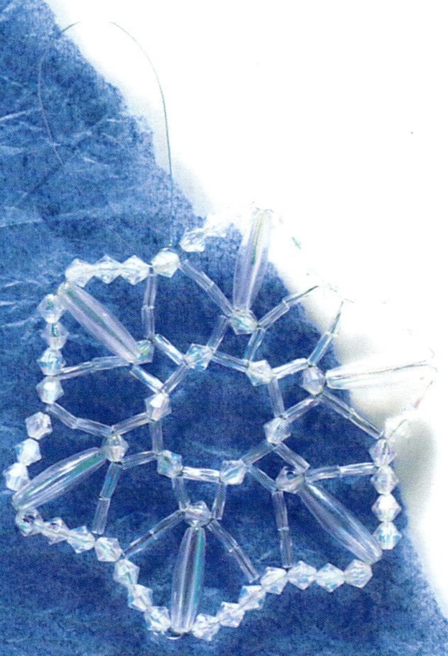

Beaded Snowflake B

1. Follow Steps 1-4 of **Beaded Snowflake A**, substituting faceted beads for bicone beads.

2. For large points, thread two bugle, one faceted, and two bugle beads. Thread wire through faceted bead on next medium point. Thread two bugle, one faceted, and two bugle beads. Thread wire through faceted bead on next small point. Double back through two bugle beads and continue pattern until snowflake is completed. Thread wire through last bead twice, then through next three beads; trim excess.

3. For hanger, fold a 6" length of wire into a loop; thread one end through faceted bead on one medium point. Twist wire ends; trim excess.

Materials

- crystal twisted bugle beads (78)
- 4mm white faceted beads (30)
- 32 gauge bead wire
- wire cutters
- needle nose pliers

Beaded Snowflake C

1. Read **Beading Basics**, pgs. 58-60.

2. For center circle, work counterclockwise. Leave a 3" tail and thread six faceted beads on a $1^{1}/_{2}$ yd length of wire. Thread wire through first bead to form a circle. Twist tail around wire close to first bead; trim tail. Refer to **Beading Diagrams**, pg. 57, and thread one faceted bead to center of circle; thread wire from left to right through bead on opposite side of circle.

3. For snowflake points, thread one bugle, one faceted, and one "E" bead. Double back through faceted bead, using pliers to bend wire close to "E" bead. Thread one bugle bead. Thread wire from left to right through faceted bead on circle again. Refer to **Beading Diagrams** and thread wire through next bead on circle. Repeat pattern five more times. Thread wire through two faceted beads on circle.

4. For hanger, fold remaining wire into a loop. Twist wire end around center circle at base of loop; trim excess.

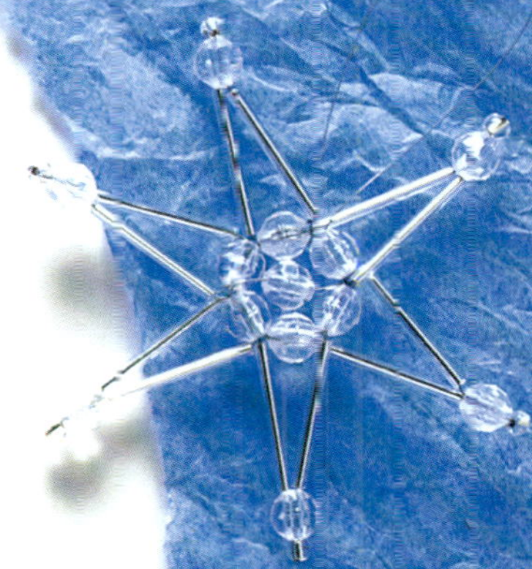

Beaded Snowflake D

1. Follow Steps 1 and 2 of **Beaded Snowflake C**.

2. For snowflake points, thread one bugle, one bicone, one bugle, one bicone, one faceted, and one bicone bead. Double back through faceted and bicone beads, using pliers to bend wire close to bicone bead at point. Thread one bugle, one bicone, and one bugle bead. Thread wire from left to right through faceted bead on center circle again. Refer to **Beading Diagrams**, pg. 57, and thread wire through next bead on center circle. Repeat pattern five more times. Thread wire through two faceted beads on center circle.

3. Follow Step 4 of **Beaded Snowflake C** for hanger.

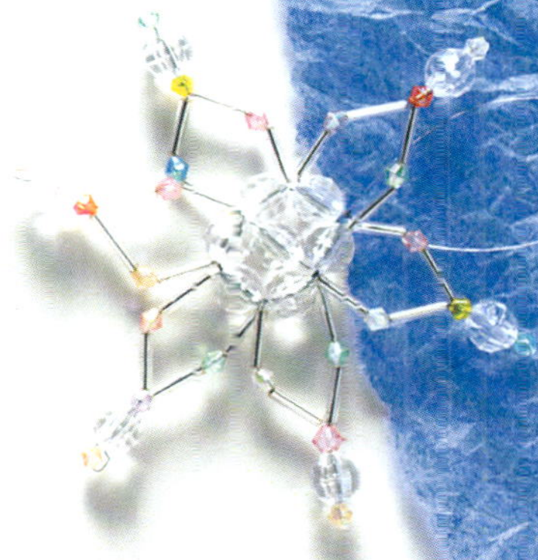

Beaded Snowflake E

1. Read **Beading Basics**, pgs. 58-60.

2. For center circle, refer to **Beading Diagrams**, pg. 57, and work counterclockwise. Leave a 3" tail and thread one round and one faceted bead on a $1^{1}/_{2}$ yd length of wire. Repeat pattern five more times. Thread wire through first round bead to form a circle. Twist tail around wire close to first bead; trim tail.

3. For snowflake points, thread one bugle, one faceted, one bugle, one faceted, one bugle, one faceted, one bicone, and one faceted bead. Double back through bicone and faceted beads, using pliers to bend wire close to faceted bead at point. Thread one bugle, one faceted, one bugle, one faceted, and one bugle bead. Thread wire from left to right through round bead on center circle again. Thread wire through next faceted and round beads on center circle. Repeat pattern five more times.

4. Follow Step 4 of **Beaded Snowflake C** for hanger.

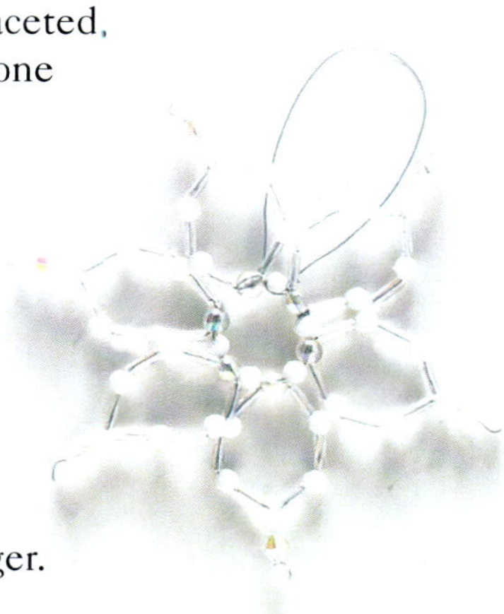

Materials

- 32 gauge bead wire
- wire cutters
- needle nose pliers

Additional Materials

For Beaded Snowflake C:

- 8mm crystal faceted beads (13)
- 25mm silver bugle beads (12)
- silver "E" beads (6)

For Beaded Snowflake D:

- 8mm crystal faceted beads (13)
- silver bugle beads (24)
- 4mm multicolored transparent bicone beads (24)

For Beaded Snowflake E:

- 5mm transparent round beads (6)
- 4mm white faceted beads (42)
- crystal twisted bugle beads (36)
- 4mm transparent bicone beads (6)

Glass Heart

1. Read **Beading Basics**, pgs. 58-60.

2. Leaving a 3" tail and locking first bead in place, thread one gold bead on a 1 1/2 yd length of thread. Thread 2 1/2" of beads, alternating crystal, frosted, and gold beads. Add one large mahogany bead and 14 gold beads. Double back through mahogany bead to form a loop.

3. Thread another 2 1/2" of beads, ending with a gold bead. Thread needle through gold bead twice to lock in place. Secure thread ends.

4. For additional tassel strand, double a 12" length of thread and tie onto tassel below mahogany bead. Repeat Step 3. Slip loop over hanger on ornament.

Materials

- clear glass heart ornament
- gold seed beads
- crystal and frosted bead mix
- large mahogany bead
- beading needle
- beading thread
- liquid fray preventative

Note: We used Blue Moon crystal and mahogany bead mixes and fine ash thread.

Glass Pear

Read **Beading Basics**, pgs. 58-60. Follow **Glass Heart** instructions, substituting bronze and mahogany beads for gold and frosted beads.

Materials

- clear glass pear ornament
- bronze seed beads
- crystal bead mix
- mahogany bead mix
- beading needle
- beading thread
- liquid fray preventative

Note: We used Blue Moon crystal and mahogany bead mixes and fine ash thread.

Glass Ball

1. Read **Beading Basics**, pgs. 58-60.

2. For center circle, work counterclockwise. Cut a $1^{1}/_{2}$ yd length of thread, adding new thread as needed. Leaving a 3" tail and locking first bead in place, thread one medium crystal bead and three gold seed beads. Repeat pattern five more times. Thread needle through locking bead twice to secure first row; place on ornament.

3. For dangles, thread one pebble bead from mahogany bead mix, one bugle bead, one pebble bead, and one seed bead. Double back through pebble bead and remainder of dangle. Thread needle from left to right through medium crystal and two seed beads on center circle. Thread a $2^{1}/_{2}$" dangle of beads with a mix of seed, crystal, gold, and mahogany beads, ending with a teardrop bead from gold bead mix. Double back through beads on dangle. Thread needle from left to right through second seed bead on center circle. Thread through one seed bead and one medium crystal bead on center circle. Repeat entire dangle pattern five more times.

4. Thread needle through next seed bead twice to lock in place. Secure thread ends to complete collar.

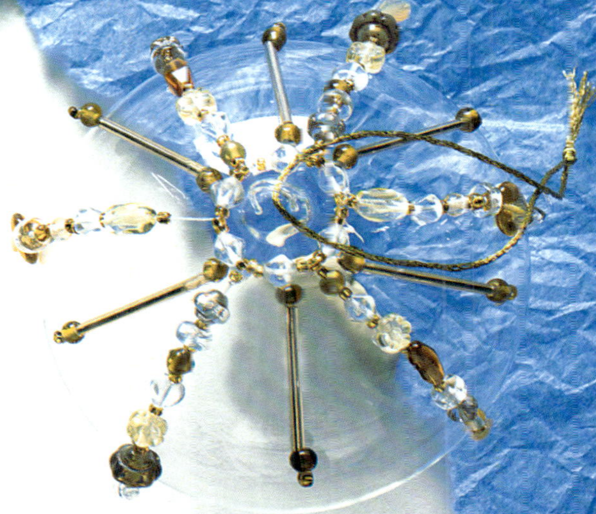

Materials

- clear glass ball ornament
- crystal bead mix
- gold bead mix
- mahogany bead mix
- gold seed beads
- 1" gold bugle beads
- beading needle
- beading thread
- liquid fray preventative

Note: We used Blue Moon crystal, gold, and mahogany bead mixes and fine ash thread

Beaded Icicles

Read **Beading Basics**, pgs. 58-60. Cut approximately 15" of wire for each icicle. Form a 5" loop, twisting end around wire to secure. (For a beaded hanger, thread 2mm pearl beads onto loop before securing wire.) Thread beads on wire, using larger beads at top and alternating with smaller beads or sequins. To finish, coil or wrap wire end to secure beads; trim excess.

Materials

- ❖ assorted pearl beads
- ❖ crystal beads of various shapes
- ❖ assorted silver beads
- ❖ assorted silver bugle beads
- ❖ 28 gauge silver wire
- ❖ large silver metallic sunburst sequins
- ❖ wire cutters
- ❖ needle nose pliers
- ❖ nail or skewer

Materials

- assorted clear glass beads
- 5mm rainbow round beads
- 20 x 22mm birthstone teardrop diamond bead
- 8mm rhinestone rondelle bead
- 13.5 x 6.5mm crystal AB teardrop bead
- 24 gauge silver wire
- wire cutters
- needle nose pliers
- pencil

Coiled Icicle

Read **Beading Basics**, pgs. 58-60. Thread birthstone teardrop bead onto a 24" length of wire. Twist wire around birthstone teardrop bead to secure. Thread rhinestone rondelle bead, covering end of wire. Thread rainbow round beads and assorted glass beads to make a 20" strand. Thread crystal teardrop bead; wrap wire end to secure beads. Loosely coil middle section of beaded icicle around pencil. Bend top of beaded strand to form hanger.

Materials

- assorted clear glass beads
- 5mm rainbow round beads
- 20 x 22mm birthstone teardrop diamond beads
- 8mm rhinestone rondelle beads
- 13.5 x 6.5mm crystal AB teardrop bead
- beading needle
- beading thread
- household cement
- liquid fray preventative

Note: We used Blue Moon fine ash thread.

Crystal Icicle

1. Read **Beading Basics**, pgs. 58-60.
2. Cut a $1^{3}/_{4}$ yd length of thread. Leaving a 3" tail and locking first bead in place, thread 2" of assorted glass beads and one rainbow round bead to complete first half of hanger.
3. For icicle, lay thread along one side of birthstone teardrop bead, then thread through bead. Dot the top, bottom, and side of birthstone teardrop bead with household cement to hold thread in place; allow to dry.
4. Thread one rhinestone rondelle bead, one rainbow round bead, 1" of assorted glass beads, and one rainbow round bead.
5. Repeat Steps 3 and 4. Thread one glass bead and one crystal teardrop bead.
6. Double back through beads, threading needle around opposite side of each birthstone teardrop bead, and stopping after last rainbow round bead. Dot the remaining side of each birthstone teardrop bead with household cement to hold threads in place; allow to dry.
7. To complete hanger, thread 2" of assorted glass beads. Thread needle through locking bead twice to form loop; secure thread ends.

New Traditions

We've given some old Christmas favorites a new twist! These contemporary classics are sure to become a holiday tradition in your home.

Santa

1. Read **Beading Basics**, pgs. 58-60.

2. For Santa's face and hat, refer to **Beading Diagrams**, pg. 57, and use Crisscross Method to thread beads from Rows 1-12 onto a 48" length of 36 gauge wire.

3. For Row 13, thread six red "E" beads onto left end of wire, then bring wire ends together and thread six red "E" beads, one 7mm pearl bead, and one 2mm pearl bead onto both wires. Coil each wire, thread green beads, and coil wire ends to secure beads; trim excess.

4. For Santa's whiskers, cut fourteen 10" lengths of 26 gauge wire. Refer to **Beading Diagrams** to thread one wire between two rows at side of face; fold in half and twist to secure. Thread assorted size pearls onto each half of wire, coiling wire where desired. Trim to various lengths; wrap wire ends to secure beads. Continue around sides of face and beard, adding wires between rows as needed and between beads on Row 1.

5. For hanger, loop a 10" length of monofilament around Row 13 wire; knot ends.

Materials

- 4mm pearl beads (16)
- 4mm red faceted glass bead (1)
- 4mm rose faceted glass beads (21)
- 7mm red round glass bead (1)
- black "E" beads (2)
- 6mm pearl beads (7)
- red "E" beads (62)
- 7mm pearl bead (1)
- 2mm pearl bead (1)
- assorted green beads (3)
- assorted pearl beads
- 36 gauge silver wire
- 26 gauge white coated wire
- monofilament
- wire cutters
- needle nose pliers
- nail or skewer

Candy Cane

1. Read **Beading Basics**, pgs. 58-60.

2. Cut a 12" length of red wire and wrap one end to secure beads. Thread beads on wire, alternating red and pearl beads for approximately 8". Wrap wire end to secure; trim excess. Bend wire into a candy cane shape.

3. Cut a 15" length of green wire and wrap one end to secure beads. Thread green and lime beads on wire. Wrap wire end to secure. Tie beaded strand in a bow and secure to candy cane with a small length of green wire.

4. For hanger, loop a 10" length of monofilament between beads at top of candy cane; knot ends.

Materials

- 7mm pearl beads
- assorted red and green beads
- lime seed beads
- 18 gauge red metallic wire
- 24 gauge green metallic wire
- monofilament
- wire cutters
- needle nose pliers

Wreath

1. Read **Beading Basics**, pgs. 58-60.

2. Cut a 12" length of green metallic wire. Leaving a 1" tail, thread holly leaf bead on wire; coil wire on both sides of leaf to secure bead. Continue threading leaf beads in this manner, adding red or green beads where desired. Twist wire ends together to form wreath.

3. Cut a 20" length of light green wire. Leaving a 1" tail, thread green beads on wire, coiling wire where desired. Wrap light green beaded wire around wreath wire, twisting ends to secure.

4. Cut a 12" length of red metallic wire; shape into a bow. Cut a 9" length of red metallic wire; wrap around bow and wreath. Twist ends to secure.

5. For hanger, loop a 10" length of monofilament around wire at top of wreath; knot ends.

Materials

- green holly leaf beads
- red "E" beads
- assorted green beads
- 22 gauge green metallic wire
- 24 gauge light green wire
- 18 gauge red metallic wire
- monofilament
- wire cutters
- needle nose pliers
- nail or skewer

Teardrop Angel

1. Read **Beading Basics**, pgs. 58-60.

2. Cut a 24" length of wire. For head, thread one "E" bead onto wire. Fold wire in half and thread both ends through faceted bead, one "E" bead, and disc bead.

3. For wings, thread 28 assorted beads on each wire end. Thread both ends back up through center beads, bending wings into shape. Trim excess wire at top "E" bead.

4. Cut a 24" length of wire. Thread one end through top bead and wrap to secure. Bend wire to form hanging loop; twist loop just above top bead to secure. Thread wire end through center beads. Thread teardrop bead and double back through center beads. Twist wire around bottom of hanging loop to secure. Leaving a 6" tail, trim excess. Curl tail to form halo.

Materials

- clear silver-lined "E" beads (2)
- 15mm clear faceted bead (1)
- 11mm disc bead (1)
- assorted beads (56)
- 2" acrylic teardrop bead (1)
- 26 gauge copper bead wire
- wire cutters
- needle nose pliers

White and Gold Angel

1. Read **Beading Basics**, pgs. 58-60.

2. For halo, cut a 1 1/4 yd length of wire. Thread one gold bead, one red bead, and one pearl round bead to middle of wire; repeat pattern three more times. Thread wire end through first four beads again, bending wire into a circle.

3. For head, bring wire ends together and thread faceted bead, berry bead, and one pearl round bead on both wires.

4. For each wing, thread one pearl oval bead on one wire. Thread one gold bead, one red bead, and one pearl round bead; repeat pattern four more times. Bend wire into a circle; thread wire through pearl oval bead again.

5. For skirt, refer to **Beading Diagrams**, pg. 57, and use Crisscross Method to thread beads from Rows 1-7 onto wire ends. For Row 8, thread three gold beads on each wire. Thread one gold bead on one wire. Double back through last two beads; trim excess. Thread remaining wire through center gold bead. Double back through last two beads; trim excess.

6. For hanger, twist ends of a 6" wire length around halo wire to form a loop; trim excess.

Materials

- 5mm gold round beads (33)
- 7mm red pony beads (14)
- 5mm pearl round beads (31)
- 6mm clear faceted bead (1)
- 20mm berry bead (1)
- 6mm pearl oval beads (2)
- 26 gauge copper bead wire
- wire cutters
- needle nose pliers

Red Icicles

Read **Beading Basics**, pgs. 58-60. Cut one 15" length of wire for each icicle. For hanging loop, leave a 1" tail and thread 2" of beads onto wire, alternating seed beads and pebble beads. Thread one large bead, then 2" of seed beads and pebble beads in reverse sequence. Bend beaded wire to form loop; twist end of loop around wire to secure and thread larger beads, then smaller ones to desired length. Wrap wire end to secure beads; trim excess.

Materials

- ❖ red seed beads
- ❖ red glass pebble beads
- ❖ assorted red beads
- ❖ 28 gauge silver wire
- ❖ wire cutters
- ❖ needle nose pliers

Materials

- ❖ 3" dia. Styrofoam™ ball
- ❖ red crystal bicone bead
- ❖ red crystal faceted bead
- ❖ red glass pebble beads
- ❖ green bugle beads
- ❖ green frosted glass beads
- ❖ upholstery needle
- ❖ beading needle
- ❖ 10" square of ivory fabric
- ❖ rubber band
- ❖ red and gold braid
- ❖ gold loop braid
- ❖ metallic gold floss
- ❖ beading thread
- ❖ liquid fray preventative
- ❖ 3/4" gilt sequin pins
- ❖ craft glue
- ❖ hot glue gun

Holly Ball

1. Read **Beading Basics**, pgs. 58-60.

2. Gather fabric around ball, smoothing fabric folds. Wrap rubber band around gathered fabric. Trim excess fabric at top of rubber band. Using six strands, wrap floss tightly around rubber band, hot gluing floss in place as needed.

3. For hanger, thread upholstery needle with one 15" length of floss. Knot one end to secure beads; trim excess. Thread faceted bead, then bicone bead. Hot glue knot to top of gathered fabric and hot glue beads together. Separate strands and knot floss ends together; trim excess. Wrap and glue additional floss around gathered area as needed.

4. Hot glue braids to fabric at base of hanger.

5. For berries, load seven pins with one pebble bead; pin to ball to make berry clusters.

6. For each leaf, thread beading needle with a doubled 1 yd length of thread; knot ends. Use needle to catch fabric close to a bead; thread two bugle beads. Repeat pattern seven more times to form a leaf shape, ending near beginning bugle bead.

7. Continuing with same thread for leaf center, thread three bugle beads, catch fabric with needle, and thread three or four bugle beads to finish at point of leaf. For added shape, couch between each pair of beads, running thread under fabric between stitches. Knot end of floss; trim excess. Dot beginning and ending knots and thread ends with liquid fray preventative.

8. Load five pins with one green frosted bead; pin to ball to fill gaps between leaves and at ends of leaves. Adjust pins as desired and secure.

Pomegranate, Peach, And Pear

Read **Beading Basics**, pgs. 58-60. Separate sprays, in order to work with a single fruit. Remove leaves and set aside. Place a bead on a sequin pin and press into fruit, using needle nose pliers if necessary. Continue adding beads and pins close to one another but not touching, until entire fruit is covered. When beading is complete, hot glue leaves to stem; wrap entire stem with floral tape. Tie ribbon in a bow around stem.

Materials

- pomegranate (small spray)
- pear (small spray)
- peach (small spray)
- gold transparent rainbow seed beads
- $^{7}/_{8}$"w gold ribbon (18" length per ornament)
- $^{1}/_{2}$" sequin pins (approx. two packages per fruit)
- green floral tape
- needle nose pliers
- hot glue gun

Top

Read **Beading Basics**, pgs. 58-60. Paint top gold; hang to dry. Load several pins with one bead and sequin. Pin to top around hanger. Pin four rows of loaded pins around center of top. Load several pins with one bead; pin one row along top of center section and fill gaps along bottom of beaded section near hanger. For dangle, thread one bead to center of a $2^{1}/_{2}$" length of wire. Fold wire in half and thread both ends alternately through beads and sequins, ending $^{1}/_{4}$" from wire ends. Push ends of wire into center bottom; dot with hot glue to secure.

Materials

- 3" papier-mâché top
- gold seed beads
- 34 gauge gold wire
- $^{1}/_{2}$" sequin pins
- gold round sequins
- gold metallic acrylic paint
- paintbrush
- wire cutters
- hot glue gun

Large Star

Read **Beading Basics**, pgs. 58-60. Paint star gold; hang to dry. Load five beads on each corsage pin and pin to points of star. Load several sequin pins with one bead and sequin. Pin to star along raised edges, slanting pins as needed. Insert more loaded pins where desired.

Materials

- 4" papier-mâché star
- assorted seed beads
- corsage pins (5)
- 1/2" sequin pins
- assorted round sequins
- gold metallic acrylic paint
- paintbrush

Bell

Read **Beading Basics**, pgs. 58-60. Paint bell gold; hang to dry. Load several pins with one bead and sequin. Pin to bell around hanger. Pin two rows around bottom edge of bell and one row to bottom of bell. Pin columns of four loaded pins around bell. Load several pins with one bead; pin three loaded pins to continue each column and fill gaps along edge of beaded section near hanger.

Materials

- 3" papier-mâché bell
- assorted seed beads
- 1/2" sequin pins
- assorted round sequins
- gold metallic acrylic paint
- paintbrush

Small Star

Read **Beading Basics**, pgs. 58-60. Paint star gold; hang to dry. Load several pins with one bead and sequin. Pin to star along raised edges, slanting pin as needed.

Materials

- 3" papier-mâché star
- green seed beads
- 1/2" sequin pins
- gold round sequins
- gold metallic acrylic paint
- paintbrush

Red Star

1. Read **Beading Basics**, pgs. 58-60.

2. For star, leave a 1" tail and thread one spaghetti bead and one dark red bead onto chenille stem. Bend stem to form inner corner of star. Thread one spaghetti bead and one dark red bead. Bend outer corner.

3. Repeat pattern four more times.

4. For hanger, twist ends together to form a small loop.

Materials

- spaghetti beads (10)
- dark red transparent silver-lined glass beads (10)
- 3mm x 12" gold tinsel chenille stem

Metallic Star

1. Read **Beading Basics**, pgs. 58-60.

2. For star, attach 10mm rings to split ring. Leaving a 1" tail, thread one gold bead, five red beads, and one 10mm ring onto chenille stem. Bend stem to form inner corner of star. Thread five red beads. Bend outer corner.

3. Repeat pattern four more times. Thread stem through first gold bead.

4. For hanger, twist ends together to form a small loop.

Materials

- 8mm gold beads (5)
- dark red transparent silver-lined glass beads (50)
- 10mm gold washed rings (5)
- 16mm gold split ring (1)
- 3mm x 12" gold tinsel chenille stem

Simple Star

1. Read **Beading Basics**, pgs. 58-60.

2. For star, leave a 1" tail and thread beads approximately 3/8" apart onto chenille stem. Bend stem at 1" intervals to form inner and outer corners of star.

3. For hanger, twist ends together to form a small loop.

Materials

- dark red transparent silver-lined glass beads (25)
- 3mm x 12" gold tinsel chenille stem

Gold Ball Star

1. Read **Beading Basics**, pgs. 58-60.

2. For star, leave a 1" tail and thread one red bead and one 10mm bead onto chenille stem.

3. Skip approximately 3/8" and thread one red bead, one 6mm bead, and one red bead, bending stem at the 6mm bead to form inner corner of star. Skip approximately 3/8" and thread one 10mm bead. Bend outer corner. Repeat pattern three more times.

4. Skip approximately 3/8" and thread one red bead, one 6mm bead, and one red bead, bending stem at the 6mm bead to form inner corner. Thread stem through first two beads.

5. For hanger, twist ends together to form a small loop.

Materials

- dark red transparent silver-lined glass beads (11)
- 6mm gold beads (5)
- 10mm gold beads (5)
- 3mm x 12" gold tinsel chenille stem

Big Red And Gold Star

1. Read **Beading Basics**, pgs. 58-60.

2. For star outline, leave a 1/2" tail and thread beads onto one chenille stem. Bend stem at 1" intervals to form inner and outer corners of star. Twist ends together.

3. For star center, twist one end of remaining stem around one inner corner of star. Thread two evenly-spaced beads onto stem; twist stem around next inner corner. Repeat pattern four more times; do not trim.

4. For hanger, thread five evenly-spaced beads on stem. Twist end of stem around hanger to form a small loop; trim excess.

Materials

- dark red transparent silver-lined glass beads (110)
- 3mm x 12" gold tinsel chenille stems (2)

Red And Gold Egg

1. Read **Beading Basics**, pgs. 58-60. Spray paint egg and allow to dry.

2. For tassel, cut a 22" length of thread. Thread one 3mm bead; lock in place. Thread one 8mm faceted bead and one star sequin. Thread enough 3mm beads, red bugle beads, and rondelle beads to make a $5^1/_2$" beaded strand. Thread one star sequin, one 8mm faceted bead, and one 3mm bead. Lock last bead in place and secure thread ends.

3. Repeat Step 2 with a 21" length of thread, using enough beads to make a $4^1/_2$" beaded strand, and with a $19^1/_2$" length of thread, using enough beads to make a 3" beaded strand.

4. Cut a 16" length of wire; fold in half. Thread both ends through one rondelle bead and 18mm faceted bead, leaving a loop below rondelle bead. Slip three tassel strands through loop so they dangle at different lengths; pull wire taut. Twist wire ends together. Push wire through egg from center bottom to center top, pulling at top until faceted bead touches bottom of egg. For hanger, form a small loop and twist wire ends to secure; trim excess.

5. For egg, load twelve 2" pins with one 8mm bead, three 3mm beads, one star sequin, and one round sequin; pin evenly around egg.

6. Load 115 of the $^3/_4$" pins with one 3mm bead, one star sequin, one gold bugle bead, and one 3mm bead. Load fifty $^3/_4$" pins with one 3mm bead, one 6mm bead, and one tri-bead. Load fifty $^3/_4$" pins with one 3mm bead and one 8mm bead.

7. Randomly push loaded $^3/_4$" pins into egg.

8. Adjust pins as desired and secure.

Materials

- 3" dia. Styrofoam™ egg
- 3mm gold seed beads
- 8mm red faceted beads
- 5mm gold bugle beads
- 5mm red bugle beads
- 6mm gold rondelle beads
- 18mm red faceted bead
- 11mm red tri-beads
- beading needle
- 20 gauge gold wire
- gold metallic thread
- liquid fray preventative
- 2" gold sequin pins
- $^3/_4$" gold sequin pins
- 6mm gold star sequins
- 8mm red round sequins
- gold floral glitter spray paint
- transparent tape

Green And Gold Ball

1. Read **Beading Basics**, pgs. 58-60. Spray paint ball and allow to dry.

2. For beaded strand, cut a 30" length of thread. Thread one 5mm bead; lock in place. Thread three 3mm beads, one oval bead, three 3mm beads, and one 5mm bead; repeat pattern eight more times. Lock last bead in place and secure thread ends.

3. Pin first locking bead to ball. Pull bead strand around ball; pin end bead to top of ball near first locking bead. Load several sequin pins with one bicone bead; pin to ball along either side of bead strand, holding strand in place.

4. For hanger, cut a 20" length of thread. Thread one 5mm bead; lock in place. Thread one oval bead and one 5mm bead; repeat pattern nine more times. Lock last bead in place and secure thread ends. Pin locking beads to top of ball.

5. For ball, load 32 pins with one 4mm green bead, one round sequin, and one snowflake sequin; pin randomly around ball.

6. Load 70 pins with one bicone bead and 70 pins with one 4mm gold bead and one bicone bead; pin randomly around ball.

7. Adjust pins as desired and secure.

Materials

- 3" dia. Styrofoam™ ball
- 5mm green round beads
- 3mm green round beads
- 3 x 6mm green oval beads
- 4mm crystal bicone beads
- 4mm green round beads
- 4mm gold round beads
- beading needle
- beading thread
- 3/4" gold sequin pins
- 8mm gold round sequins
- 24mm green snowflake sequins
- gold floral glitter spray paint
- liquid fray preventative

Red, Green, And Gold Egg

1. Read **Beading Basics**, pgs. 58-60.

2. Holding trim end at top of egg, wrap trim lengthwise around egg, making ten even sections. Form a 3" loop of trim at top of egg; push 2" pin through entire thickness into egg. Trim excess; dot end of trim with glue.

3. Wrap trim around middle of egg, overlapping ends. Fold top end under and dot with glue. Wrap trim around top and bottom half of egg and secure.

4. For egg, load 30 silver pins with one silver bead and pin where trims intersect on side of egg. Load gold pins with one red or green bead. Fill in sections of egg, alternating bead colors.

5. Adjust pins as desired and secure.

Materials

- 3" dia. Styrofoam™ egg
- 6mm silver round beads
- 4mm red and 4mm green transparent "E" beads
- 3 1/3 yds of 1/4"w gold trim
- 2" gold sequin pin
- 3/4" gold and 3/4" silver sequin pins
- craft glue

Beading Materials

seed beads
frosted glass beads
petite glass beads
round beads
pebble beads
faceted beads
ring beads
needle nose pliers
sequins
tri-beads
bead mixes
wire cutters
wooden beads
spaghetti beads
berry beads
coated wire
bead wire
jewelry wire
copper wire

Beading Diagrams

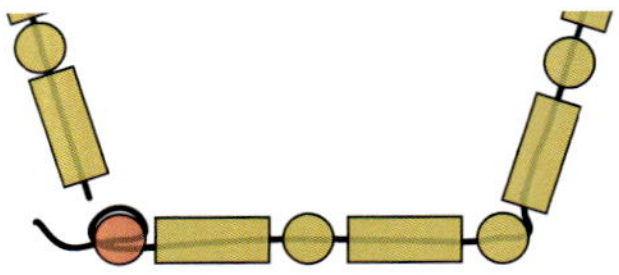

Row 1

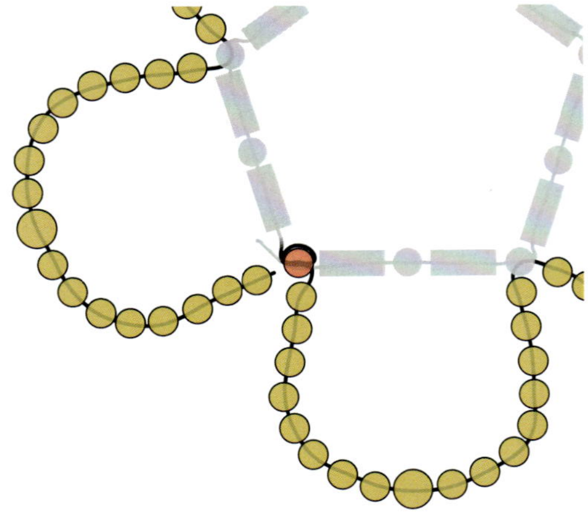

Row 2

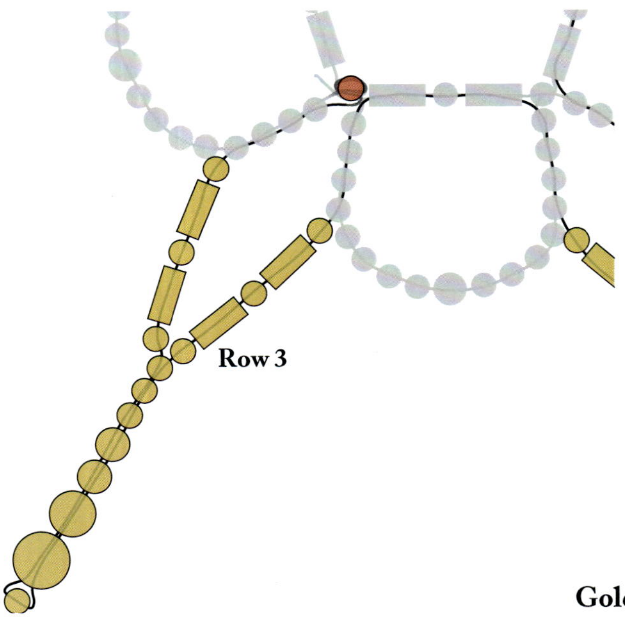

Row 3

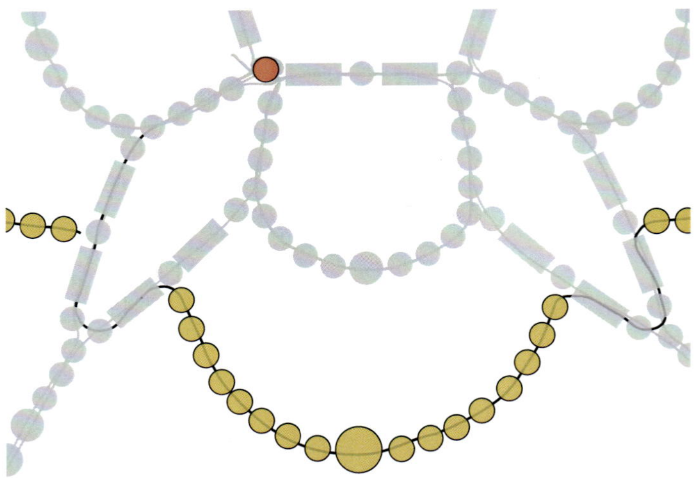

Row 4

Gold Collar

Note: Red bead indicates beginning locking bead.

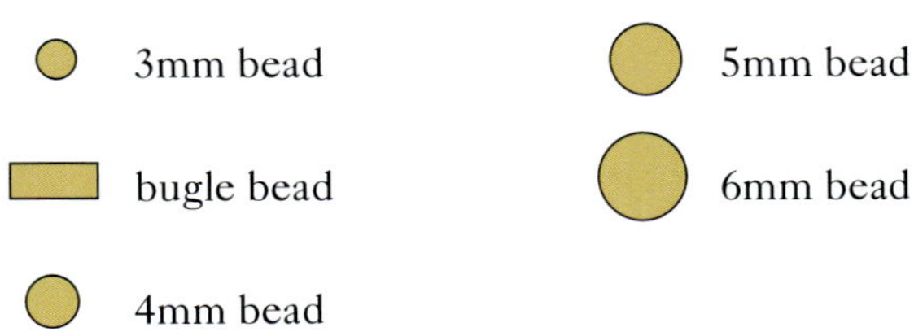

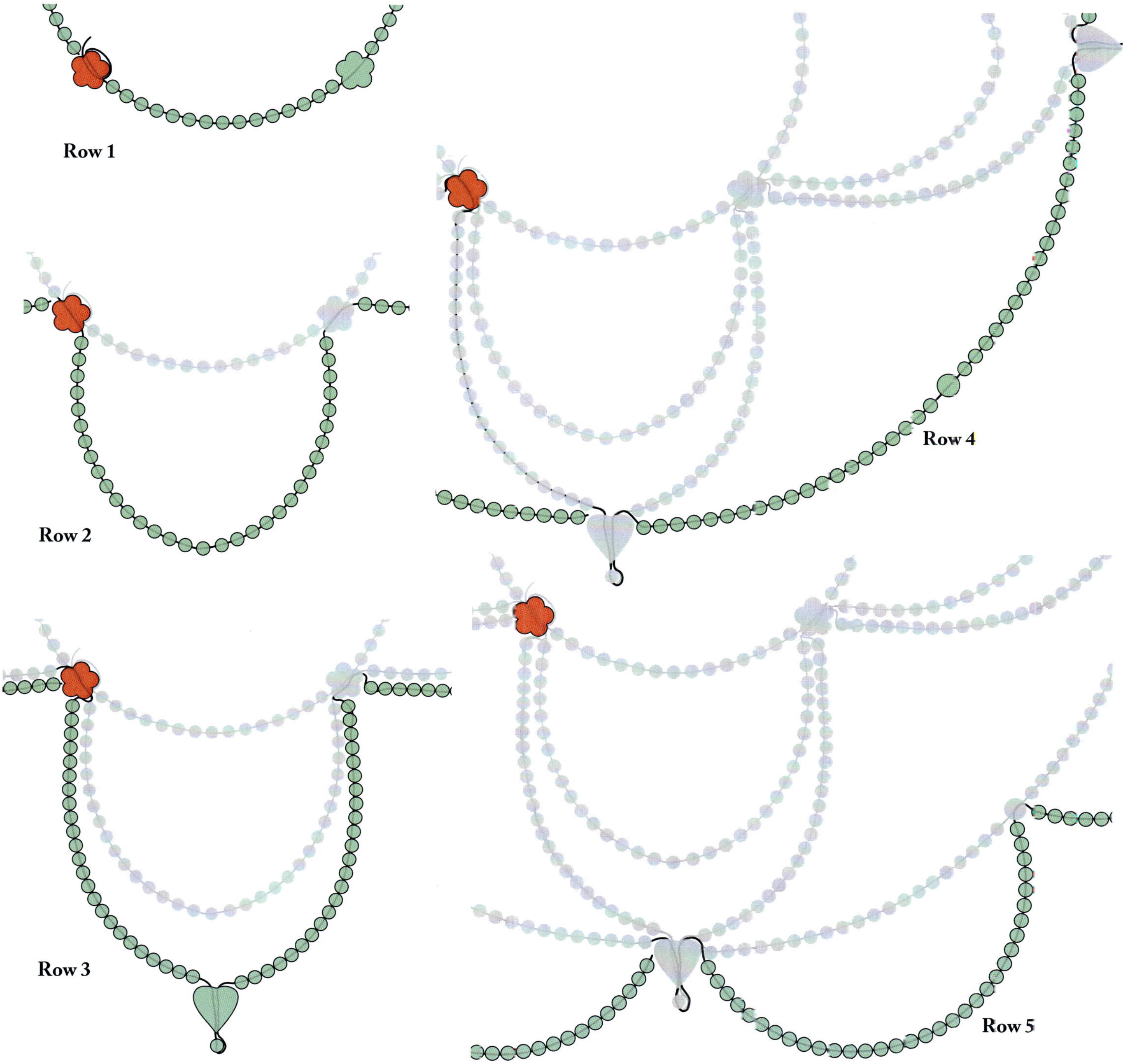

Green and Gold Collar

Note: Red bead indicates beginning locking bead.

Row 1

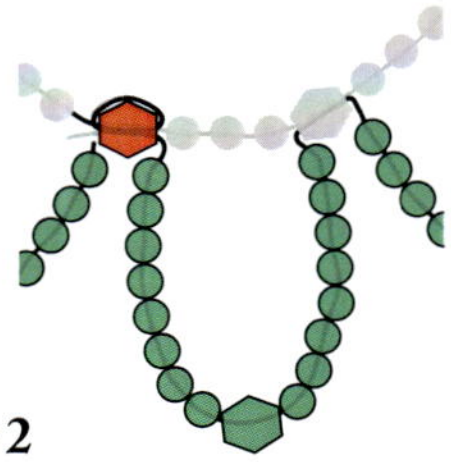

Row 2

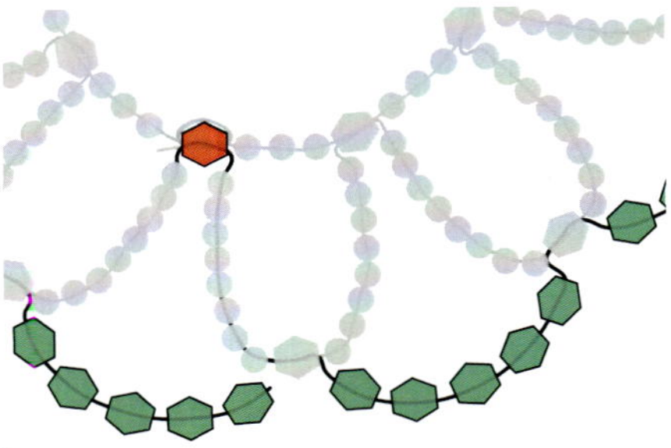

Row 3

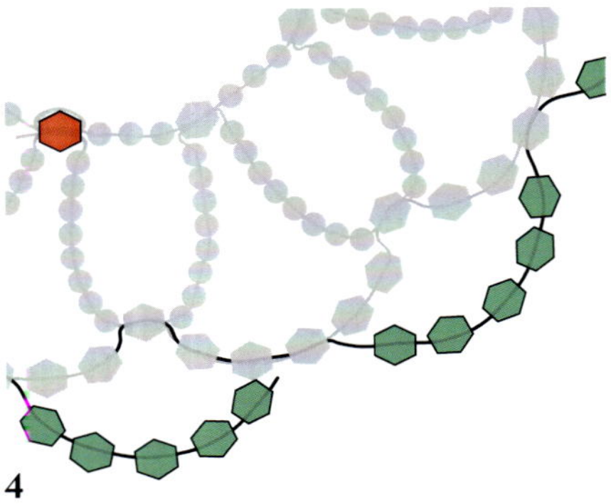

Row 4

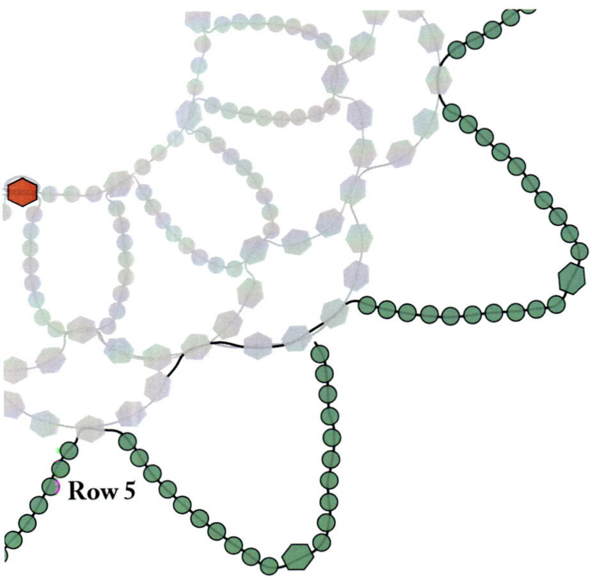

Row 5

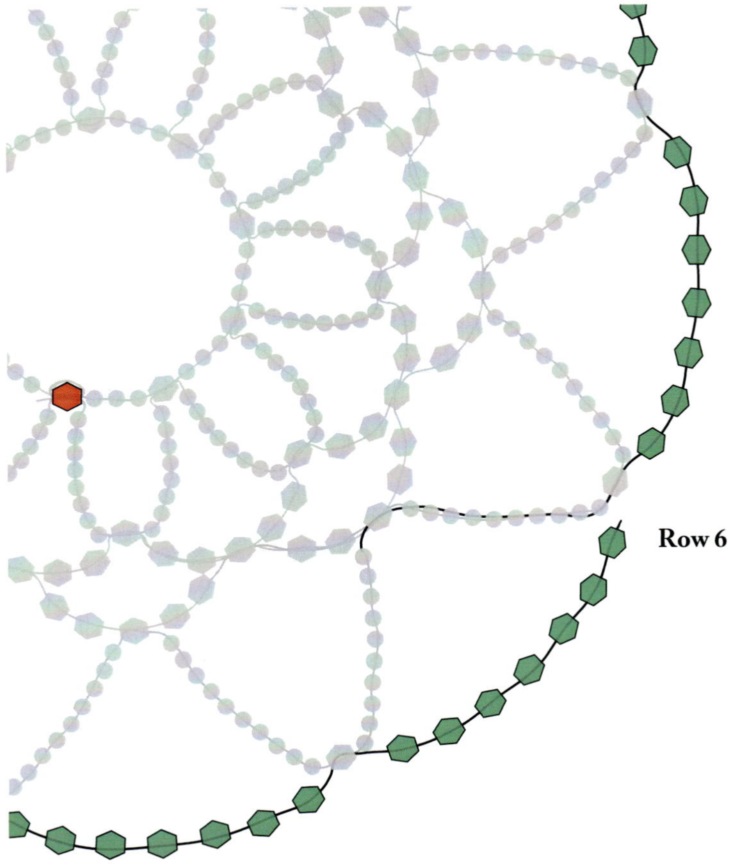

Row 6

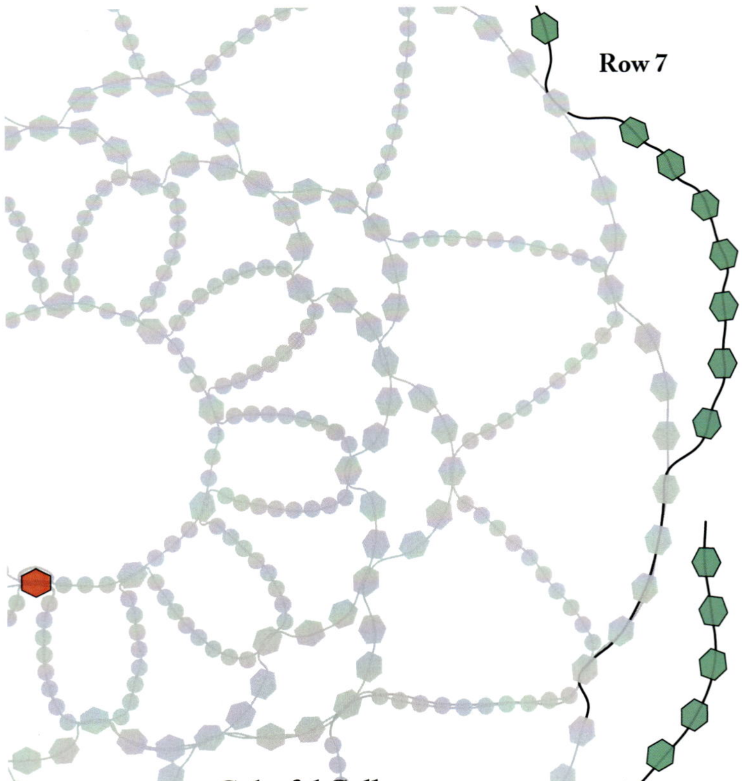

Row 7

Colorful Collar

Note: Red bead indicates beginning locking bead.

bicone bead   seed bead

Long Dangle

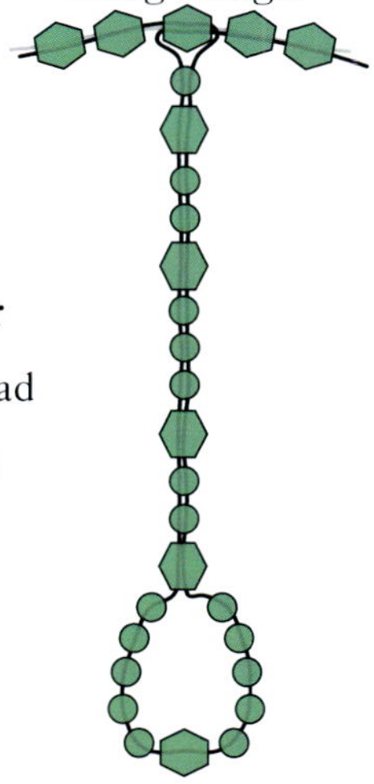

Colorful Collar

- bicone bead
- seed bead

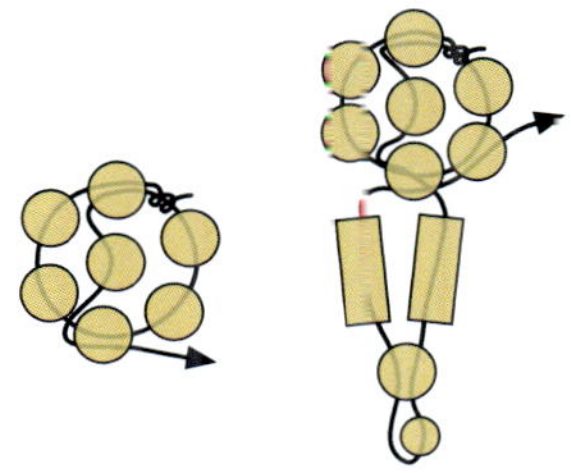

Beaded Snowflake C

- faceted bead
- bugle bead
- "E" bead

Small Purse

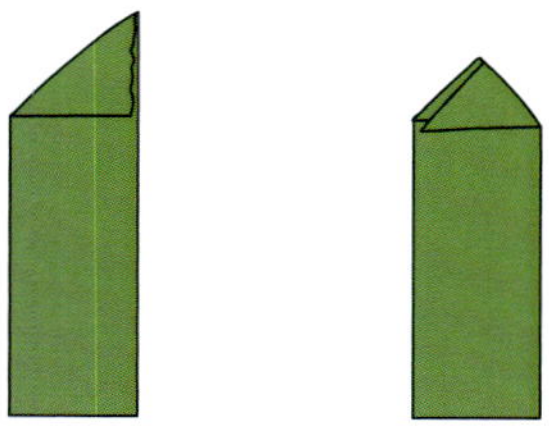

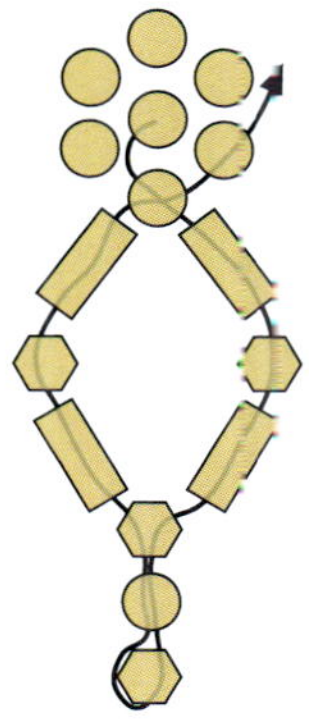

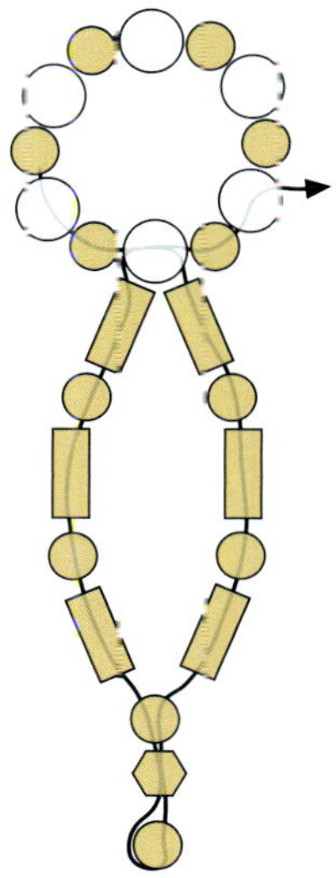

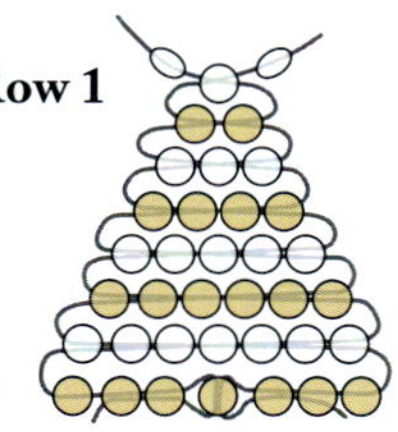

White And Gold Angel

- 5mm gold bead
- 5mm pearl bead
- 6mm pearl oval bead

Beaded Snowflake D

- faceted bead
- bugle bead
- bicone bead

Beaded Snowflake E

- faceted bead
- round bead
- bugle bead
- bicone bead

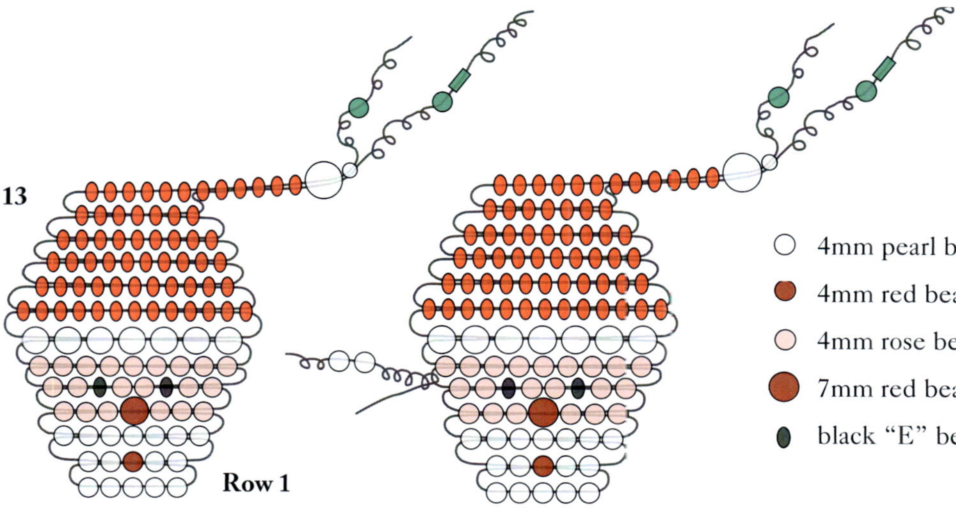

Santa

- 4mm pearl bead
- 4mm red bead
- 4mm rose bead
- 7mm red bead
- black "E" bead
- 6mm pearl bead
- red "E" bead
- 7mm pearl bead
- 2mm pearl bead
- assorted green beads

Beading Basics

BEADING TIPS

Refer to Beading Materials, pgs. 52 and 53, to identify the types of beads and other supplies that we used to create our ornaments.

To develop the different styles in this book, we chose beads from many different manufacturers. The Materials list that accompanies each project includes the size and number of most beads. When the bead size is not included, work with beads of your choice.

For designs where a certain size bead is needed to complete the project, such as beaded collars, use the same size beads as listed in Materials, or adjust the number of beads as needed to complete the ornament.

We found that with some types of beads, such as "E" beads, sizes may vary within a package and the number of beads may need to be adjusted.

Place beads on a paper plate, bowl, or chamois cloth. To keep from dropping beads, thread beads directly from the plate onto needle, wire, or pin.

Pick up several beads on needle before moving them onto the thread. With practice, this is a real time-saver, too!

To hold ornament steady when working with beaded collars, place ornament in a paper cup.

BEADING ON PINS

There are many colors and types of pins that can be used in beading ornaments. Some pins have heads that add to the design, while others blend with the beads.

Eye Pins And Head Pins

Eye pins and head pins are bendable and work well with wire to create dangling shapes. Load pin with beads and use needle nose pliers to wrap the end of the pin around wire, or thread wire through the eye of the eye pin.

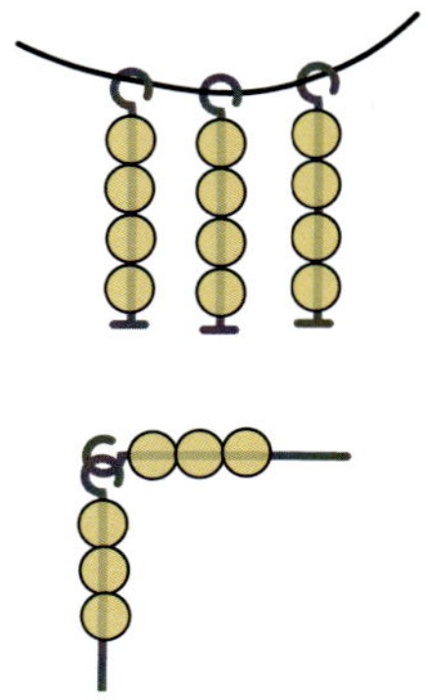

Securing Pins

Load beads on pins and push pins into Styrofoam™ ornaments. After determining final placement of pins, remove one at a time from ornament, dip tip into craft glue and reinsert into ornament to secure pins.

BEADING WITH THREAD

Choose from a variety of beading needles and threads to create beautiful collars and to bead on fabric. We recommend that you work with beading thread, which is stronger than sewing thread. Be sure to use a size needle and thread that will pass through the smallest bead in your ornament without putting stress on the thread.

Threading Needle

Thread beading needle with one **doubled** strand of thread unless otherwise indicated in project instructions. It may be helpful to tape the tail to a table as you begin threading beads.

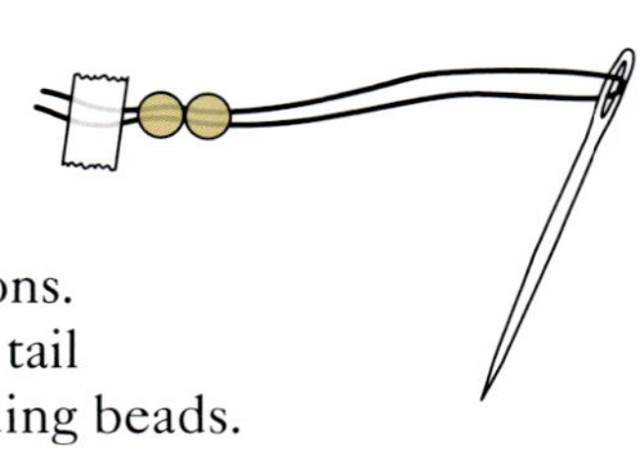

Locking Bead

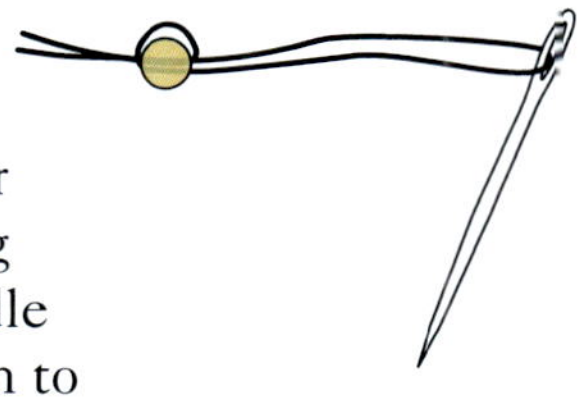

A locking bead at the beginning of a strand keeps the beads from sliding off your thread. Leaving a 3" tail, string first bead on thread. Pass needle around and through bead again to lock in place. Thread beads as indicated in project instructions. Locking beads are also used at the end of a thread or dangle.

Securing Thread Ends

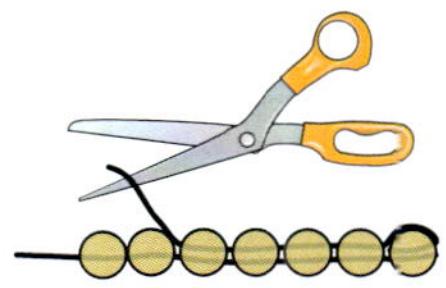

To secure an ending thread, lock last bead in place and double back through last four beads; unthread needle, leaving a tail. Add new thread to continue strand (see below), or trim tail and dot locking bead and thread end with liquid fray preventative.

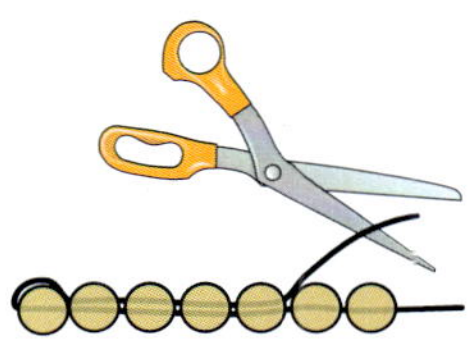

To secure a beginning thread, rethread needle with beginning tail. Pass needle around locking bead and through next four beads. Trim tail and dot locking bead and thread end with liquid fray preventative.

Adding Threads

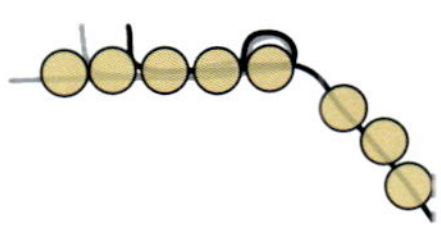

To add thread, pass newly-threaded needle through the last three beads on the strand, leaving a 3" tail. Thread needle through last bead twice to lock in place and continue beading. Trim tails and dot locking bead and thread ends with liquid fray preventative.

EMBROIDERY STITCHES

Follow the stitch diagrams to bring the needle up at odd numbers and down at even numbers, adding beads as indicated in project instructions.

Beaded Backstitch

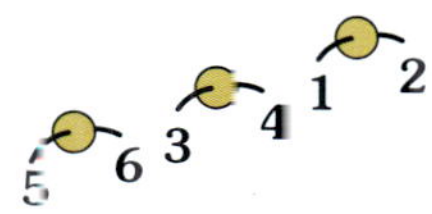

Couching

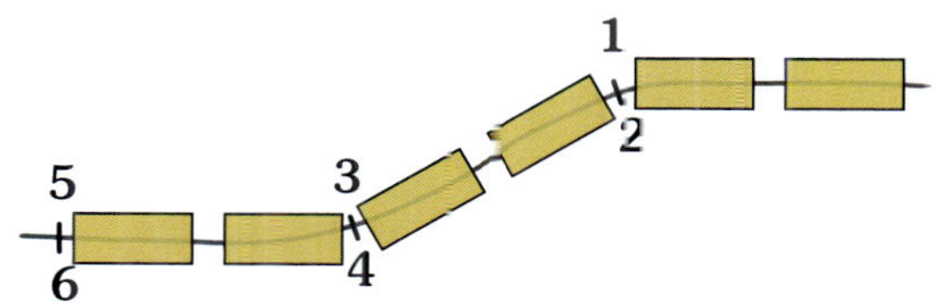

Overhand Stitch

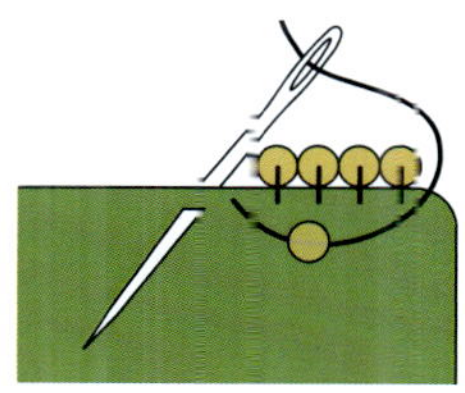

BEADING WITH WIRE

Beading wire is available in many colors and gauges and may be used to enhance the style of your project.

Coiling Wire

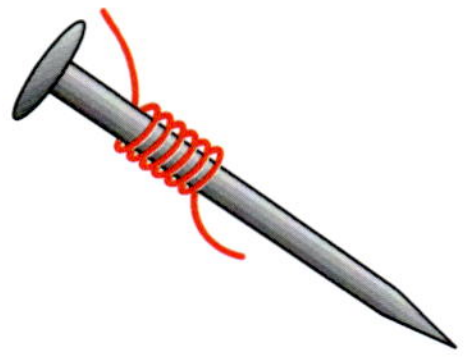

Coiling wire ends is one way to secure beads and coiling the wire between beads will add a playful look to your project. Use needle nose pliers to wrap wire around a nail, skewer, or T-pin, or make a cone-shaped coil by wrapping wire around a tapered paintbrush.

Curling Wire

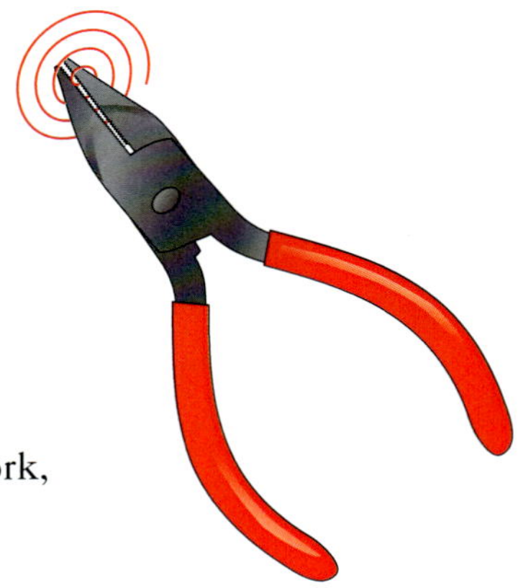

Curling the wire ends is a decorative way to secure beads. Grasping one end of the wire with needle nose pliers, rotate the wire around pliers to curl. The closer to the tip of the pliers that you work, the smaller the curl.

Wrapping Wire Ends

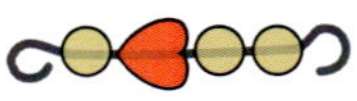

In many projects, wire ends are wrapped to secure beads. Use needle nose pliers to bend wire, rounding the end into a tight loop.

Crisscross Method

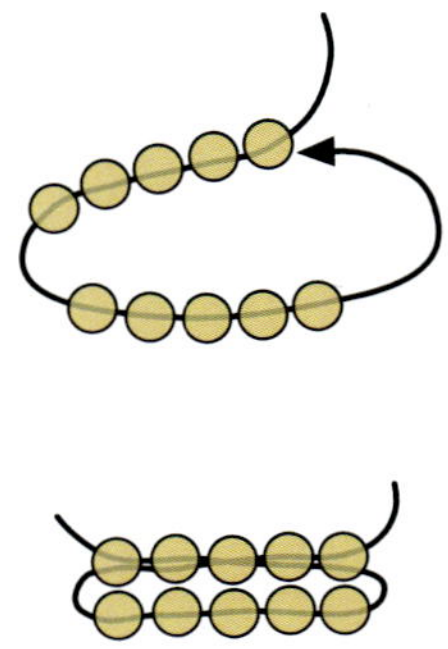

Thread and center a row of beads onto a length of wire. Bend wire ends toward center for next row. Thread next row of beads onto one end of wire. Run other end of wire through beads, crisscrossing wires. Continue adding rows, crisscrossing wires by threading through opposite ends of beads.

Made in U.S.A.

We would like to extend thanks to Therm-O-Web of Wheeling, Illinois, for providing us with PEELnSTICK™ sheets and tape and to Wire Art of Underhill, Vermont, for donating coated colored wire and tools used in making our ornaments.

Production Team: Designers – Cherece Athey, Diana Cates, Becky Werle, Anne Stocks, Peggy Cunningham, Polly Browning, and Linda Tiano; Editorial Writer – Suzie Puckett; Technical Writers – Joyce Holland and Laura Sia Holyfield; Production Artists – Lora Puls, Dana Vaughn, and Ashley Carozza; Photography Stylist – Cassie Newson Staff Photographer – Russ Ganser; Pattern Tester – Judy Millard